The

Vagabond Book

of

Stirling

Marie Brammeld

Stirling: Lomax Press, 2010

Stirling: Lomax Press, 2010
First edition, 2010
ISBN: 978-0-9560288-3-9

Copies of this book may be obtained directly from Lomax Press. Enquiries to:

lomaxorders@btinternet.com

Contents

Acknowledgements:

The Vagabond Book was a totally unexpected result of a family history course run by Stirling Council Archives, and would never have been produced had I not been inspired by the original 18th century leather-bound, handwritten copy, which contains many more stories than those selected here.

My thanks must go in the first instance, therefore, to the Stirling Archivist, Pam McNicol, for her hard work and professionalism in preparing the course material. Thanks also to Archive staff Jane, Barbara and Michael, who cheerfully made me welcome while I transcribed the entries.

My gratitude also extends to Dr Elspeth King, Curator of the Stirling Smith Art Gallery and Museum, for her friendly encouragement and practical help, along with permission to use several illustrations shown throughout the book.

I have one other person to thank: my part-time technical adviser, part-time practical support system and full-time husband, Forbes. If patience is a virtue he must truly be a saint. I have yet to find a project quirky enough for him to raise even one eyebrow.

The Vagabond Book Of Stirling:

1752- 1787

Introduction

The Vagabond Book of Stirling is a rogues' gallery of sorts, a genuine historical record of misdemeanours and punishments kept by the magistrates of the Burgh of all the ne'er-do-wells to be hauled before them. A selection of their stories are told here.

Vagabonds are loosely defined as vagrants, drifters, tramps, itinerants, shifty-double-dealers without any visible means of support. They were considered, at best, to be disreputable and a nuisance to society. Then again, those recorded in *The Vagabond Book of Stirling* are hard to define in such a strict sense, (some had homes, others had employment) so the definition of 'vagabond' remains loose.

All of them, however, were definitely up to no good, and were hauled before the town magistrates to account for themselves.

The crimes were largely petty in nature, rather than those which would be tried in a more serious court of law, ranging from theft, breach of the peace, and assault and battery to general socially unacceptable behaviour. Loose morals featured heavily, given the nature of the times, and - as ever - women came off by far the worst.

Punishment was swiftly administered – a miscreant could be apprehended by the Town Guard, thrown in the Tolbooth overnight, appear before a Baillie in the morning, and be whipped out of town by noon the next day.

The legacy of *The Vagabond Book* is to leave us a unique slice of Stirling's social history, showing us what life was really like up the crowded vennels at the Top of the Town in the 18th century, and often hinting at what went on behind the doors of the more fashionable residences, too.

In addition, the human stories of *The Vagabond Book* are placed in their social and historical context, and so will prove of interest to both the casual reader and those looking for a local history book with a difference ...

Setting the Scene

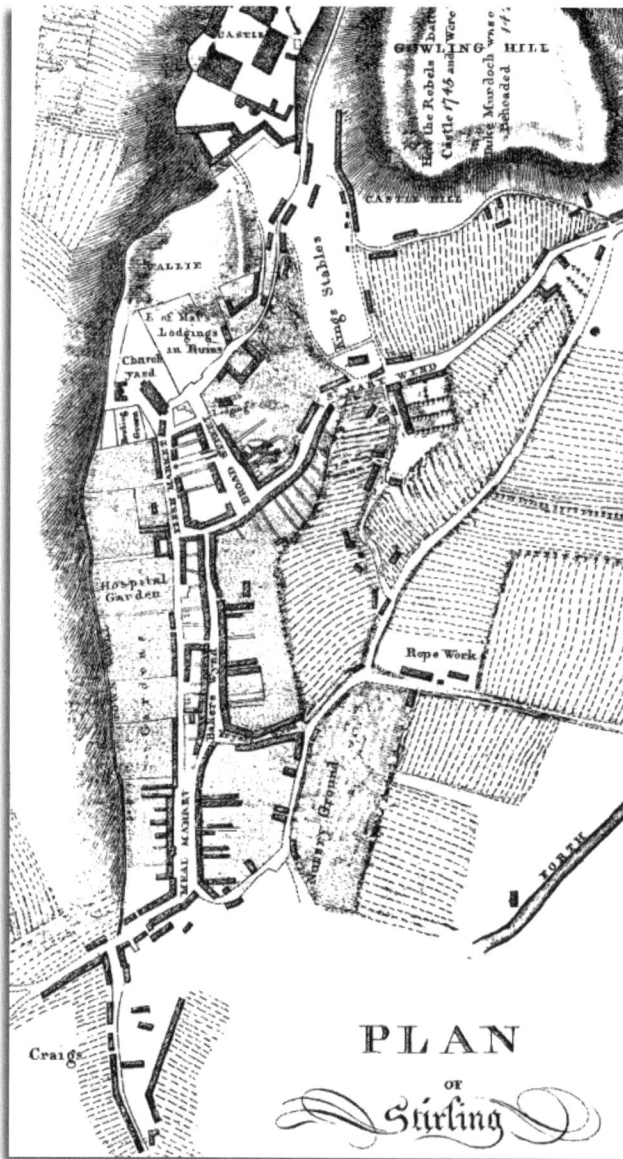

Charles Ross:
Plan of Stirling, 1780

What were living conditions like in 18th century Stirling?

Well, life could be summed up in three words: cramped, noisy and smelly.

The majority of people lived in the crowded tenements lining the narrow and congested roads leading up to the Castle, in all, around 4,000 people living in an area about two miles long and half-a-mile wide.

St. Mary's Wynd was especially gruesome.

At one point it was said to be only 14ft wide.

The other main streets were Port Street, Friars Wynd, Quality Street (now King Street), Baxters Wynd (now Baker Street), Broad Street, and the Back Raw (now St. John Street/Spittal Street).

The better streets would have been cobbled, but the others would simply have been bare earth – pretty squishy underfoot after a good soaking from our Scottish weather.

At the side of the buildings fronting the streets, passageways or 'closes' gave access to areas behind the houses, where vegetables were grown, or pigs or hens kept. Indoors, there were no facilities such as toilets, or even basic running water.

People queued at the woefully few water pumps to fill their pails or pitchers, then heaved it back to their homes. Once there, not a single drop was wasted. The same water used for washing could just as easily swill down steps.

Sewage, along with offal from slaughtered animals, was simply thrown into the street, to lie, rotting and exposed, until the next shower of rain washed it downhill to the foot of the town into what is now Murray Place. At that time it would simply have been a filthy, contaminated bog. Its nickname at the time was 'The Stank', which says it all.

So that's the place. Now let's meet the people.

Martha Ferrier

Case 1   **4ᵗʰ December 1752**

Martha Ferrier has the dubious distinction of being the first vagabond to appear. Her waywardness is recorded forever, one early winter's day in 1752.

Martha had been employed as a servant to a Mr Walter Allan and his family, but lasted only about ten days before running away. Mr Allan was probably glad to see her go, as *she proved a very bad servant* as well as spending most of her time cavorting with the local soldiers.

What he was decidedly less pleased about, however, was that she ran off in his very own shoes. She was brazen enough, too, when seen making off in them by two of Allan's children, James (17), and Bridget (11), to insist the shoes were an old pair, which they *knew to be false*.

Well, the magistrates having considered all the evidence,

'find it proven that the said Martha Ferrier is a loose vagabond and disorderly woman, and can give no proper account of herself, and haunted the company of soldiers, and that at all hours of the day and night for sometime bygone and from which acts of wickedness and uncleanness is presumed, and that she was also guilty of dishonesty in her service'.

Unfortunately we don't know what happened to Martha after that, but we certainly know a great deal about Mr Walter Allan ...

Twenty years earlier, on the basis of an essay titled '*The Hilt of a Cutlass*' he was admitted Freeman of the Incorporation of Hammermen at Stirling, and five years later became their Deacon.   Today he is still regarded as one of the most skilful sword-hilt makers in Scotland, along with his father, John, and brother John Jnr. They specialised in 'basket hilts', which would enclose and protect the hand grasping the sword.

Basket hilt made by James Grant, apprentice to Walter Allan

(Photo courtesy of the Stirling Smith Art Gallery and Museum)

A great deal of their business was conducted with the Highland clans, and in a letter to an Edinburgh craftsman employed to put the finishing touches to a batch of their sword-hilts, the Allans asked him to hurry, as their clients were clamouring for the order to be delivered.

The date? Just before 1745.

After the 1745 Rebellion the Government were so determined to stamp out mutinous Scots they introduced an Act which outlawed both the wearing of Highland dress and the bearing of any instruments of war. This law was so strictly enforced by Major-General Wade that it virtually ended the use of swords in Scotland.

It's likely that Allan then manufactured hilts for the Highland Regiments in the British Army, who were exempt from the new law.

A Load of Rubbish

Case 2   **4th December 1752**

James Kirkland, son of a Chelsea Pensioner, was foolish enough to try his luck at thieving from one of the Baillies himself.

' ... he went in by the window to Baillie Henderson's hay-loft, where he found a pair of men's shoes which he designed to carry off, but John Reid, the servant, coming in, the declarant was apprehended and discovered ...'

Not only that, he had done much the same thing before.

'Declares that he was bred a Weaver, but has not followed that business for a long time bygone, and has had his chief support since by running errands for the Fleshers. Acknowledges that some weeks ago he went by a window into the hay loft of James Bryce and found there a holster pistol and a pair of gloves of a Dragoon Drummer's quartered there for a night in their way south, which pistol and gloves he carried off undiscovered, and hid in the rubbish at Mar's Work, and also a pair of garters and buckles and a razor, and when apprehended ... he told where these were, and were found.'

Mar's Wark

The well-known ruin glowering above Broad Street was built around 1570 for the Earl of Mar, who needed to be near his day job at the Castle – he was Regent of Scotland, after all, as James VI was only just over a year old when he became King.

According to the Burgh Records, the building was used as a barracks after 1715 before being taken over by the Town Council in 1733, who had plans to convert it into a workhouse. It was badly damaged during the second Jacobite Rebellion (1745-6) before finally falling into ruin.

Not that this would have surprised Daniel Defoe, who visited Mar's Wark in 1723 and left a worried man. He was far from happy about its close proximity to the Castle. Surely, in the event of a battle, Mar's fine building would be badly damaged?

His fears were realised in 1746. It was.

Six years later, our James Kirkland is busy hiding his ill-gotten gains deep in its rubble.

Bowie The Butcher

Case 3   **20th October 1754**

'Mary Whitehead, who was this day confined to the workhouse for being accessory to a riot committed by some soldiers upon James Bowie, flesher, … and for stealing of a gill stoup[1] out of the said James Bowie's house, and said Mary Whitehead being examined by the Baillie owns that she came to this place about 4 weeks ago with the companies of General Stewart's Regiment of Foot quartered here, that since that time she has stayed and cohabited with Joseph Dean, a soldier in the said Company as man and wife though she owns they are not married, as not having had time to be so....

Declares she was born at Manchester, and followed the Regiment to Scotland from Wigan.'

Eee, Mary, chuck, you *are* in trouble. There were witnesses –

---

[1] A measuring jug: a stoup is a tankard, a gill is a measure of volume (1/4 pint.)

'Janet Haugh, spouse of John Wallace, tailor in Stirling declares that on the night of the 25th being alarmed with a noise in the said James Bowie's house, she came from the next house thereto, and saw 3 soldiers above James Bowie beating and abusing him, and also saw Mary Whitehead now at the bar with a gill stoup in her hand that belonged to the said James Bowie, beating him about the head, and she the declarant took the said stoup out of Mary Whitehead's hand, and knew it to be James Bowie's, and the Guard having come Mary Whitehead went off when the soldiers were secured.'

'Janet Burgess, servant to Janet Edmond, brewer in Stirling, declares that on the night of the 25th upon hearing a noise in James Bowie's house, she came to the door and saw several soldiers above James Bowie beating and abusing him in his own house. She saw Mary Whitehead also in the house with the soldiers, and the Guard having been called and come to the said house, Mary went off and the soldiers were carried to the Guard.'

'William Bowie, apprentice to James Bowie, declares that on the night of the 25th, Mary Whitehead came to his master's house 3 different times about buying a piece of beef, that the 3rd time 3 soldiers attacked James Bowie and threw him to the ground, and having got above him they cruelly beat and abused him, and Mary Whitehead being also present the 3rd time, the declarant saw her attack Isobel White, spouse to the said James Bowie, and tear the clothes off from her head, and beat her upon the face and shoulders with her fists, and the Guard having been called, Mary Whitehead went off and the soldiers were carried to the Guard.'

We don't know what punishment the soldiers received, but the Baillie (would you believe a Mr Robert **Bowie**?) had no hesitation in deciding

'Mary Whitehead to be recommitted to the workhouse, there to remain till liberated in due course of law.'

The Workhouse

In 1672 an Act was passed authorising all Scottish Burghs to erect a Workhouse, or "House of Correction", in which vagrants and beggars could be ordered by Magistrates to be detained against their will and set to work. This usually consisted of picking oakum, or stone-breaking if the sentence was hard labour.

The Deported Drover

Case 4   **11th July 1752**

'*John McMartin says he lives in McMartin's Country in Lochaber; he came to the fair of Stirling drivering cattle for McDonald of Gallachie, that in the Chapmen's creams[2] upon the forestreet of Stirling upon Tuesday last the Fair Day he was buying a horn comb from one of the chapmen, and at same time stole out of his cream the six folding knives and the two dozen yellow metal buttons that were found upon him and now produced in court, and having been in liquor he owns that he stole the other particulars time and place foresaid from different chapmen, and which were also found upon him and now produced in court … 6 bone combs, garter strings, 6 pair of stockings, 3 blue bonnets, 4 and a half yards tartan plaid, and also owns he took a piece of white cloth out of George Grahame, Chapman, and that he was followed by the said George Grahame, who took the cloth from him.*'

About six weeks later his case comes up again, this time with an astonishing conclusion.

'*.. the said John McMartin to avoid a trial for the crimes foresaid hereby voluntarily banishes himself from the Kingdom of Scotland in all time coming during his lifetime, and compeard William McAdam, Burgess of Glasgow for and in name of William Lary, shipmaster in Glasgow and Company, and hereby enacts himself to transport the said John McMartin to one or other of His Majesty's Plantations in America, and to report a certificate from the proper officer of having landed him there under the penalty of 20 pounds in case of failzie[3].*'

So John McMartin, a Highland cattle drover, came to the Stirling Fair one late autumn day. His journey from Gallachie (approximately 50 miles north-east of Inverness) would have taken him several weeks. He would often have to spend the night out in the open beside his cattle, wrapping his plaid around him for warmth. Some of his meals may only have been oatmeal mixed with cold water.

Eventually he reached Stirling. Presumably he made a successful sale at the Fair, enough to buy a good few drinks, at any rate. But then his life changed forever.

---

[2] market-stalls
[3] failure to carry this out

Caught stealing from the market stalls, he spent six weeks in the Tolbooth – a bad enough experience – and was then transported to an American Plantation.

Presumably the outcome of the pending trial would have been worse, so he chose the lesser of the two evils.

Chapmen

So who were the chapmen, selling *'all manner of things'* at the Stirling Fair?

Chapmen were essentially the mobile shop of their day. They travelled the countryside, buying and selling a wide assortment of goods. Some kept to their local hamlets and farms, carrying their goods on a huge pack on their backs, but those who owned a horse travelled much farther, and were able to carry a much greater load. Local fairs and markets were popular selling-places, and some hired a stall for the occasion. (The local cooper would make some money by constructing a basic wooden framework for a booth, then hiring it out when needed.) But the chapman was more than a mere hawker of goods. He also played a valuable role in circulating the news of the day.

Physically, the lonely routes and the nature of their loads made them easy targets for robbery, and extortion money was sometimes extracted to guarantee a safe passage. There could be self-inflicted dangers, too, due to the weight of their enormous packs. When they stopped to rest on a dyke, the pack could tumble to the other side, pulling the thick shoulder strap up around the hapless owner's neck and choking him to death.

As with any other business, debtors could be a problem. One Highland chapman tramped miles to collect his debt from the local laird. He was made very welcome, and was delighted to be wined, dined, and invited to stay the night. Looking out his window the next morning, however, the smile died from his lips. He was horrified to see a dead body swinging from a rope. When informed by a servant it belonged to a local merchant who had pressed the laird for payment, the chapman took to his heels and fled for his life.

Needless to say, the laird looked pretty smug when taking down his straw dummy.

He'd be able to use it on yet another occasion.

"... Some Small Children."

Case 5   **11 June 1755**

Margaret Ross had already been banished the year before, but had re-entered Stirling and been discovered. Baillie James Jaffray must have been in a reasonable mood that fine June morning, for he allowed his finer feelings to prevail *'in respect she has some small children'.*

However, he was not altogether a soft touch. If she was discovered in the town again,

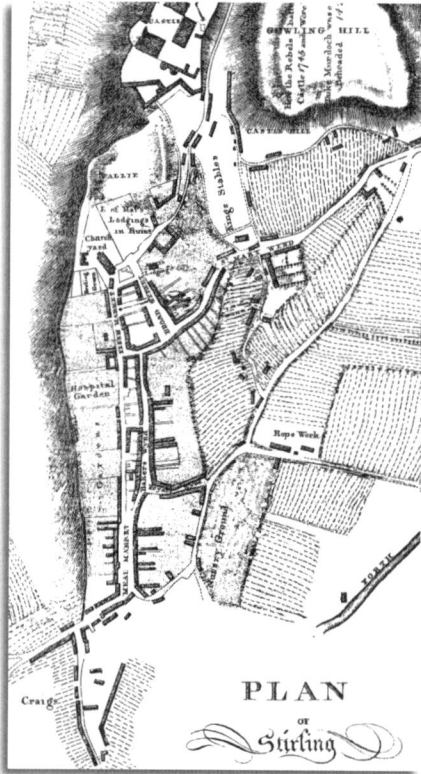

Extent of town in 1780

'she will be again committed to the workhouse at hard labour for the space of three months and publickly whipped by the hands of the common Hangman through the Burgh the first Friday of each month, and the last of these Fridays to be burnt on the face and again banished.'

Burgh boundaries

It's hard for us to imagine the choices facing a young mother with 'several small children' being banished from her home.

It should be remembered, though, that Stirling in the 18th century was a much smaller place than today, stretching roughly from the Castle down to what is now the main shopping centre.

This would have been a double-edged sword for Margaret – on the plus side, she was not obliged to travel very far from her home to be technically outside the burgh, but at the same time her chances of being discovered if she re-entered would have been reasonably high.

Two of a Kind

Case 6   **11th February 1756**

'Janet Edmond, who was taken up upon Sabbath last for lewd and indecent practices, and who being examined declares that she is ane unmarried woman and bore a bastard child in March last, and has been out of service since, and is again several months gone with child, and gives George Riddoch who Writes at the Sheriff Clerk's Office as its father, and acknowledges that she was in a closed room with the said George on Sabbath last from about midday till between at four and five o clock that night, that she was discovered and secured by the constable, and declares that she has no funds of living or subsistence and that she has been maintained since her confinement with the said George Riddoch.'

Well now, young Riddoch seems to have a good enough job, so he should be able to pay for his own child. Our Baillie McKillop thought so, anyway, and ordered George and Janet

'to find sufficient cautions for freeing and disburdening the town and parish of Stirling of the child the said Janet Edmonds is going with.'

The amount? £50 Scots. Not only that, until the money was found the pair were -

'to be committed to prison till such caution is found and in the mean time allows the said Janet Edmonds her liberty till Tuesday next that she may have ane opportunity to find caution.'

What then happened to George is not recorded, but presumably Janet saw her chance and made off like the clappers, for on 10th March -

'Janet Edmond having been just now found privately kept up in a house of the Mary's Wynd, the Baillie ordains her to be committed to the workhouse for the space of 14 days and then to be put out of the town.'

But in May of the same year, the Kirk Session of the Church of the Holy Rude give their own version of the same story ...

Apparently the town constables were informed George Riddoch *'had a woman of bad fame shut up in his room with him'*, and went to Baillie McKillop for instruction. He ordered them to demand entrance *'and if this were refused to call for a Smith to force open the door'*.

The smith's professional breaking-and-entering services were not required, however, as they found the door open when they returned. When George was asked who the woman was he replied it was his wife. He was then instructed to produce his marriage lines, while Janet Edmond was to be carried to the Correction House until they were produced, *'upon which she called out to George Riddoch, will you allow me to be carried to the correction house?'*

The Baillie decided that if within the next half-hour George could find Caution for her, and could also guarantee to produce her tomorrow by ten in the forenoon under the penalty of fifty pounds Scots, she could be set at liberty. Sadly for Janet, he couldn't. So she was *'carried to prison ... and in crossing the street George Riddoch took hold of her under the arm and kissed her impudently before all present.'*

Just didn't care, did he?

George Riddoch

George was quite a lad. Again, the Kirk Session Registers of the Church of the Holy Rude suggest a wee previous bit of bother ...

It's November 1752, and something is bothering the worthy elders of the Kirk Session. They have asked George Riddoch, Writer, and John Stewart, Merchant, to appear at their next meeting. Somewhat significantly, they also want to interview James Pinkerton's servant girl, who is pregnant. Is John Stewart the father? His evidence was never heard. An officer reported to the assembled Session that John Stewart could not appear – he was already in prison. Well then, might George Riddoch be the father?

He was called, but failed to appear. He was then ordered to appear at their next meeting.

He still didn't appear, and was ordered - for the third time - to appear at the next meeting. Again George was called. Again he failed to turn up.

'The Session resolved to leave him under the scandal.'

Perhaps we can draw our own conclusions.

Janet Edmond

Now we can't be certain if our Janet Edmond is the same as the

'Janet Edmond, daughter to Robert Edmond in Blackgrange' (near Logie), who in April 1745 *'confessed herself with child by one James Nicol, servant to John Burd, Maltster in Stirling, and that the child was begot about John Forman's house in Manor'*.

The Logie Kirk Session elders duly informed their Stirling counterparts, but James Nicol *'obstinately denied any guilt'*. His nerve broke in the end though, and he finally confessed. Eventually the case was referred to the Presbytery of Dunblane.

Not that Janet seemed to learn.

In August 1755, Janet acknowledged to the Kirk Session of the Holy Rude that she had borne *'a child in the country she had brought forth five months ago, and brought up Robert Finlayson, son to commissary Finlayson, as the father, but as Mr Finlayson is not in town the affair is delayed till such time as he returns.'*

The very next year – as reported above - she's in the usual trouble again, and ends up in *The Vagabond Book* beside our very own young George Riddoch.

In July 1757 she again *'confessed she was with child'*, and this time cited John Forman's son as the father. The lad owned up. For her sins, Janet had to appear on six Sabbath days before being finally *'rebuked and absolved'* in May 1763.

Never Too Young

Case 7   **8th July 1757**

Anyone know a stroppy eleven-year old? Show them this. Tell them how lucky they are it's not 1757 –

'James Watson convicted before the magistrates of having robbed William Gilchrist upon the street of Stirling of his pocket book with five notes and a guinea therein, having been brought before the said Baillie he in respect of Watson's age being about 11 years, and his confinement for about 6 weeks past, liberates him from prison, but banishes him from the town and territories of Stirling in all time coming ..

… if he be forever hereafter found within the same he will be again committed to the workhouse at hard labour for the space of 3 months and publicly whipped through the town of Stirling by the hands of the common hangman the first Friday of each month … and will be banished under more severe penalty.'

13

We can only hope young James already lived in the neighbourhood just outside the burgh, and so received merely the equivalent of a Georgian ASBO. Otherwise it's hard to imagine a boy so young being sent away from his home and family.

The Stirling Hangman

The Hangman (or Staffman, as he was locally known) was officially appointed, and was well rewarded for his gruesome work. Over and above a regular weekly wage, he was given a free house, free clothes, and on market days was entitled to ask for a free bowl of corn from each farmer. As you will no doubt discover, though, a large proportion of his duties involved whipping miscreants out of town.

Staffmans House
(front)

He lived right beside his job –

Just behind the Tolbooth,
in fact, in a house facing into
St. John Street.

The Hangman's house

The passageway running beside and behind his house through into Broad Street and emerging at the Tolbooth was appropriately named 'Hangman's Close'.

Hangman's Close today

Loose-living Lizzie

Case 8   **26 October 1757**

Poor Margaret, we're led to think. Her father's dead, and she'd been a coal-bearer since she was seven years old. Who could blame her for having a drink and a good time with a couple of fine young soldiers?

'Margaret Brown, who was committed to the workhouse last night for being a loose woman and in company with the soldiers, being brought before the Baillie and examined, declares -

That her name is Margaret Brown, that she is daughter of Robert Brown, deceased, who was collier in Borrowstoness (Bo'ness) coal works, that since she was 7 years old she has been a coal-bearer, first in the Duke of Hamilton's coal works and for about these 5 years bygone in Lord Boyd's coal works near Falkirk, and on Friday last she left Lord Boyd's works on account of the hard labour there, occasioned by a new pits being put down, and on Friday night she came to Bannockburn where she stayed that night, and Monday forenoon she came to Stirling, and fell into company with some of the soldiers in the town, and with 2 of the soldiers drank 2 bottles of ale and a dram in the house of Mrs Whitfield.

That in the morning of the same day she went with the soldiers to a house in the Castle Wynd where they drank about 5 bottles of ale, and stayed till it was late in the night, or rather early in the morning, when she and the soldiers went to a room of John Bayne's in the Mary's Wynd where the soldiers were quartered, and she passed the night with them till about 5 o'clock in the morning.

Bottom of Broad Street, at junction of St. Mary's Wynd

Well, three weeks later, the truth comes out …

'… the foresaid woman who formerly called herself Margaret Brown, having been re-examined, declares that her true name is Elizabeth Clerk, that she is lawful daughter of the deceased John Clerk in Clackmannan, that her mother Agnes Fairlie was afterwards married to David Loudon at Falkirk, that her said mother sells ale and her stepfather is employed in the Greenland fishery.'

The Baillie decides she's a loose and disorderly woman, and banishes her.

Unfortunately Stirling Castle attracted a certain kind of lady, hoping for a handsome reward from a soldier in return for the delights of her company.

The Case of the Craigs Corn

Case 9   **24th November 1757**

Strange to think now that the Craigs area once held haystacks …

Marion had been confined to the workhouse for a couple of days for stealing corn from some stacks. Three upstanding citizens had noticed someone had disturbed the stacks lately, and had actually seen Marion making off red-handed. Whether or not this led to a sort of Neighbourhood Watch is debatable, but certainly one of them caught her in the act the very next week.

'Marion Miller, who was confined to the workhouse on the 22nd for pulling victual out of the stacks in the barnyaird in the Craigs … denied pulling any of the stacks but owned that she found corn in the Craigs nearby a barn door, which she took up and Alexander Steven, weaver, turned her back with it and caused her put it into the hole of a corn stack, and Alexander Steven and James Ogilvie in Craigs and William Leckie, burgess, having been all examined, It plainly appeared to them that the stacks in the Craigs had been lately at different times pulled and quantities of victual carried off and that the said Marion Miller was seen the last week within the barn yard carrying victual forth thereof and that she is otherwise a loose and dissolute woman.'

She's banished.

All For A Light and a Fish Supper

Case 10   **12th October 1758**

Janet McGowan's been in trouble before.

' ... Who was on the 3rd May last banished the town and county of Stirling in all time thereafter ... and who in the year 1752 was long committed to the workhouse for different acts of theft ...'

Well, she certainly hasn't learnt her lesson. Two days earlier, she was -

'found in the house of William Seton, officer of Excise in Stirling, stealing candles and hard fish.'

 Not only that, it doesn't sound as though she went quietly.

'... and George McEwen, one of the Town Officers of Stirling being examined declares he was sent for by Mr Seton to take the said Janet out of his house when he found her up in Mr Seton's garret and saw there a quantity of candles in a box; that after he had forced her out he found in her custody about a pound weight of the candles and there was a ling fish lying beside her which Mr Seton says he had before taken from her.'

This time, Janet, the Baillie has most definitely lost patience with you.

'The Baillie appoints her to be again committed to the workhouse till Friday the 20th Oct., then carried by the officers to the head of the forestreet and to be from thence whipped by the hands of the common Hangman attended by the officers to the Boroughs Gate receiving the usual number of lashes upon her naked back at the usual places and thereafter renews the former sentence of banishment.'

The Benevolent Baillie

Case 11   **17th December 1763**

Occasionally, though, the Baillie showed some leniency.

Mary Miller, who was formerly banished, was again found within the burgh and committed to the workhouse.

'The Baillie considering that Mary Miller is at present under bodily distress, and not able to undergo the punishment she deserves, he appoints her to be conveyed by the Town Officers to the Port of Stirling with the drum beating.'

The Luckless Luckiesons

Case 12   **10th March 1759**

Sometimes, too, the Magistrates would reel in more than just one little fish –

'Mary Graham who was taken up last night by the guard as being in a disorderly house kept by her mother, and in lewd company, owns she has not been in service since Lammas last, and cannot give a proper account how she has passed her time since, and that Mary Graham's mother, Jean Luckieson, is reputed to keep a bad house, the Baillies find Mary Graham to be a nuisance to society and commit her to the workhouse for 6 weeks at labour and thereafter banishes her.'

This family have obviously made themselves known to be a thoroughly bad lot -

'Jean Luckieson declares she lived in Russkie in Monteith (Port of Menteith) from infancy till Martinmas last when she came to this place and took a place in John Dollar's house, and has subsisted not so much from her own labour as from what her children procured her. The Baillies considered her notorious bad character and ill-house kept by her and that she has not resided in this parish for three years and so has not by law acquired any title to be burdensome.'

The Luckieson family

Jean Luckieson was indeed born in the parish of Port of Menteith. She was christened on 7th December 1707, daughter of Patrick Luckieson and Margaret Thomson. Her sister Anna was christened on 8th April, four years later. However, it looks like her mother may have died shortly afterwards, as a Patrick Luckieson shows up as the father of a third daughter, Agnes, christened 12 July 1719, although the mother's name is now given as Isobel Stuart. Mind you, he was quite a ladies man. According to the Kirk Session records of Port of Menteith, Patrick 'at the Burn at Ruskie' is hauled up for the sin of fornication at least twice – the first time with Isabel Stewart, in November 1718 (resulting in Agnes), and again in September 1726, this time with a Margaret Spittal.

Why Jean chose the kind of life she did is now lost in time. We do know, however, that parishes looked for any opportunity they could to avoid the responsibility of paying out to the 'undeserving poor'. Jean was therefore rejected on the grounds of 'settlement', that is, she had not lived or worked in the burgh for the allotted time. Jean, in fact, had already applied to her own native Parish for poor relief ten years earlier – in 1747 she's listed in the Poor Roll of the Port of Menteith Kirk Session Records. She obviously thought she'd have better luck moving to Stirling …

Poverty was a very real threat to the ordinary working man and his family in those days, especially if you were not skilled enough in a recognised trade or craft to belong to one of the Guilds. The only help came from charitable concerns such as Spittal's, (for members of the Seven Incorporated Trades who had fallen into poverty), Allan's Mortification, (for the education of poor boys who were sons of members of the Seven Incorporated Trades), or Cowane's, (for merchants in straitened circumstances), the church collections for the poor, and the Council's own poor fund. To make matters worse, a series of poor harvests towards the end of the 18th century led to increased poverty and famine, resulting in a dramatic influx of destitute vagrants into the town. The effect of this was so bad the Council ordered 200 Beggars' Badges to be made and issued to Stirling paupers as proof they were local people. A sharp contrast to the better times of earlier years, when, in 1744, only 40 were needed.

Three Strikes Then Out

Case 13   **10ᵗʰ March 1759**

Sadly, some people just never learn …

'Margaret Douglas was taken up about 1o'clock this morning by the guard as a street walker in company with some men who had made a disturbance, acknowledges that several years ago she deserted the town upon a warrant to apprehend her for lewd practices, and that for 6 or 7 weeks past she was put into the workhouse for the same cause and liberated by Baillie Gillespie upon undertaking not to be seen in the town again – the Baillie having considered what above with the notoriety of her bad life', she's committed to the workhouse at hard labour for 2 months, *'and thereafter banished in all time thereafter.'*

The Biggest Bed in Stirling

Case 14   **24ᵗʰ March 1759**

Oh Jean, do you *really* think the Baillie will fall for this?

'Jean Ferguson was last night committed to the Correction House by the Town Guard for being a person of bad fame and lewd behaviour and who was about the middle of said night found in bed in a house of the Mary's Wynd lying with a sergeant of a recruiting party, being brought before the magistrates of Stirling, and being examined, declares that she came to this town from Kilmahog at Martinmas last and attended the sewing school till about six weeks ago when she was married to John Robison, corporal … who lately went to Germany among the drafted soldiers. That she resided with her husband for fourteen days or thereby after the marriage as he then set out with the drafted party foresaid, and ever since has resided with her

21

sister, widow to David Farrier in the Mary's Wynd of Stirling, and acknowledges that last night she was naked in her bed in the foresaid house with Sergeant Clark in the same bed with her, but –

And here's the big 'but' –

'denies that she knew of the Sergeant being in the bed with her till the guard came in to the house about 12 o'clock said night, and found him in her bed and declares that she did not challenge the sergeant after she knew he was in the bed and wanted to conceal herself from the guard when she understood they were coming into the house; owns also that there is only one bed in the foresaid house and that sergeant Clark and a recruit were very often in the house and slept therein several nights besides the last night and that the sergeant and recruit and one of widow Farrier's children slept in the bed, and the declarant with her sister and other two children lay on the floor of the house; acknowledges likewise that Mary Graham lately banished this burgh for lewd and indecent behaviour was commonly in widow Farrier's house along with the declarant since her banishment and very often slept in said house all night and a servant of Colonel Elliot's very often visited the said Mary Graham.'

So, one of Stirling's well-known citizens was then called to give his opinion -

'James Wingate, maltman and brewer in the Mary-Wynd of Stirling, being called before the magistrates and examined, declares that for some weeks past it was currently reported in his neighbourhood that Widow Ferrier kept a bad house and harboured soldiers and other loose company, and particularly that a recruiting sergeant and a recruit had been all night in the said Widow Ferrier's house along with her and the preceding declarant Jean Ferguson, and it was said and believed by the whole neighbourhood that the foresaid sergeant and recruit were too familiar with Jean Ferguson and her sister, and their indecent behaviour gave public offence, and about 14 days ago the declarant and Robert Paterson, merchant, went to Widow Ferrier and challenged her for keeping such bad company, and she begged they would make no more words about the matter, and promised and gave her hand to them, that she should not admit or entertain any such company thereafter at late hours, but the sergeant after that challenge came to the declarant and insulted and wanted to pick a quarrel with him.

Declares that last night he was told by some of his neighbours and family, that the foresaid sergeant and recruit were in Widow Ferrier's house along with her and Jean Ferguson about 11 o'clock at night, which did not look well as the doors were shut and every thing quiet in the house; that the declarant complained thereof to Baillie Muschet, and by his orders carried the guard to Widow Ferrier's house about 12 o'clock at night, and upon knocking thereat got Widow Ferrier opening the door, at which time she was in her shirt and white coat only, and upon their going into the house they found Jean Ferguson and the sergeant together both naked in the bed, and caused the sergeant rise there from and go to his quarters at John Kidd's, and on challenging Jean Ferguson for the indecency, she wept and begged of the declarant and guard to let her alone till day light, and she would then answer for herself, and when they were in the house they saw a recruit sitting at the fireside putting on his stockings, and the declarant and guard from what they observed were of the opinion and concluded that the recruit had been lying in some part of the house with the widow, while the sergeant was lying in the bed with Jean Ferguson, and the declarant and guard carried Jean Ferguson to the House of Correction, but left the said Widow Ferrier in the house to take care of her children, and he was told this morning she has absconded and he sees her door shut.'

Oh, well, there you go.

Jean Ferguson is banished. Adam Bunting, castle soldier, acted as guarantor.

The Golden Lion

The Golden Lion, King Street

The James Wingate mentioned as a witness in the case is the same person who built Wingate's Inn – now the Golden Lion Hotel, King Street.

In 1787, Robert Burns scratched what became known as the infamous 'Stirling Lines' on a window pane. He had just visited the Castle, and had been appalled at the extent of disrepair he found.

The Town Council took exception to this sentiment - seemingly in support of the Jacobite cause - so much so that Burns returned to the Inn and smashed the offending window with the butt of his riding crop.

The Baillie and the Workhouse Baby

Case 15   **5th February 1760**

'A woman who calls herself Janet Scott and says she is spouse of William Anderson, lately a soldier in the Cameronian Reg. of Foot, but who was draughted from that regiment and sent to America, having been brought before the Baillie for having this day being the Fair day of the Burgh, taken a purse from George Morison tenant in Bandeath, out of his pocket, and being possessed of some ribbons which she dropped and supposed to be stolen in the market, and she being examined denied the charge, and the foresaid George Morison being as well as William Jaffray, merchant in Stirling, James Adam, merchant there, and John Reid examines the said George Morrison declared that in the market place the said woman came close to him and he found something slip out of his breech pocket and upon examining found he had lost his purse which was a small bladder, and immediately followed the said woman, and he and the other persons declare that they saw the woman dropped the purse or bladder with a piece of narrow black satin ribbon; which purse with the money was received by the said George Morison and the satin ribbon is lodged with the Clerk till the same be claimed.'

Janet's committed to the workhouse 'at labour' till the matter be further enquired into and considered. Ten days later the Baillie decides to get rid of her, probably worried that in Janet's case, 'at labour' might just become a bit more physical than anyone had bargained for –

'... the Baillie therefore and in respect that she appears big with child, appoints her to be liberated from the workhouse, and banishes her the town.'

He almost certainly didn't want the child to be born locally, as Janet may well have claimed poor relief for both herself and her baby.

Not only that, the child would be legally entitled to claim poor relief in later years, too.

Highland Rebel

Case 16   **5th May 1760**

'A man calling himself Duncan McPhie from Lochaber, having been brought before the Baillie suspected of being a vagrant person and concerned in enticing some of the Highland battalion in town to desert the service, and he having owned he was a common beggar and giving no satisfying account of himself ...'

Duncan's committed to the workhouse pending further enquiries. Two days later he's banished.

What was Duncan's story? Perhaps he himself was once a soldier in a Highland Regiment, but, through circumstance or character, now finds himself homeless and reduced to begging.

Perhaps he saw too much bloodshed and misery, and now seizes every opportunity to warn his fellow countrymen of the horrors of war.

His story is not told here, and we know nothing of what became of him.

The Miracle Workers

Case 17   **26ᵗʰ June 1760**

It wasn't all thieving and rowdy behaviour, though. Here's a couple who put together what must have been quite an entertaining show –

'One Peter Dalziel and Mary Gordon, whom he calls his wife, and who pretends to be deaf and dumb having been in the night betwixt Thursday and Friday last committed to the workhouse by the Town Guard as disorderly persons, having been now brought before the Baillie and it appearing from the papers in their custody that they are impostors and pretend to perform extraordinary cures ...'

So one of them pretended to be deaf and dumb, the other claimed to be able to cure ailments – presumably for a sum of money, and – hey presto – the dumb can talk again! The deaf can hear!

What couldn't be miraculously cured, however, was the Baillie's scepticism.

Or his deafness to their pleas. Both Peter and Mary were banished.

Jean, her child, John Wright, and his Mother

Case 18   10th November 1761

What became of Jean's child? What became of John Wright and his family after this scandal?

'Jean Coustone, spouse of Robert Thomson, sometime journeyman Wright of Stirling, and since at London, having been brought before the Baillie and examined, declares that it is about two years since her husband went to follow his employment at London, since which time she has constantly resided in Stirling and did not see her husband since the time foresaid he went to London, that betwixt ten or eleven months ago there was one Isobel Brugh, wife to one of the Highland soldiers, who lay with the declarant for about fourteen days while she stayed in town, and who one night while the declarant was out for ale at her desire introduced John Wright, Wright in the Baxter Wynd of Stirling a married man, who was that night upon the Towns Guard, into the declarant's bed unknown to her, and Isobel, having been in bed when the declarant returned without any ale as it was late and the houses shut, when Isobel desired the declarant to come to bed which she accordingly did, not suspecting that there was a man there in,

(oh, no, not again - just how big *were* these beds?)

but soon after on her perceiving that there was a man in bed who was making an attempt upon her, she endeavoured to get out of the bed … she then told him that he had ruined her, when he answered to her that there was no fear of that …'

Well, Jean gave birth to a baby girl in September. But the matter didn't end there. At the beginning of November –

'the wife of Andrew Hutton, coal carrier in Stirling who lived next door to the declarant, and who was often alongst with her while on child bed, and who during that time had often threatened the declarant with being turned out of her room as soon as she was able to travel, did advise the declarant that as John Wright the father had a small family of his own, the best thing she could do was to lay down the child at the door of Jean Buchanan, widow of Robert Douglas, weaver, and mother to John Wright, and Hutton's wife undertook to

lay down the child at Jean Buchanan's door as she knew the house, and the declarant having been prevailed on by her, they went together, betwixt the hours of nine and ten o clock at night on the Saturday foresaid, and the declarant carried the child to the foot on the New Street or Entry leading to Jean Buchanan's house where Hutton's wife received the child from her, went up the said New street or Entry with the child and laid it down at the door, and Hutton's wife gave the declarant half a crown to help her away, upon her getting some of the declarant effects; the declarant stayed that night in Miss Elphingstone's house and on Sunday time or after sermons she went to Newhouse and stayed that night in a change house[4] being as she thinks the Eastmost house on the left hand, and on Monday she went to Linlithgow, and next day went to Edinburgh, where she stayed and span with a woman who has a room, and being uneasy about her child she returned to this place on Thursday last.'

Who - if anyone - is telling the truth?

'Isobel Mickeljohn, spouse to Andrew Hutton, denies her giving any advice to lay down her child – she knows as being next neighbour that Jean was with child and brought forth the same, and heard that it was laid down and that thereon she had left the town; declares that the day before the birth Jean was in the declarent's house with her spinning wheel, when John Wright and his wife came in and desired Jean to give the child to the right father, for that he was not the father, when she answered that he might deny it before men, but that there was a day coming when it would not deny with him ...'

The Baillie commits Jean to the workhouse.

A Jean Buchanan or Wright married a Robert Douglas on 17 Aug 1755, in Stirling.   Previously, a Jean Buchanan and an Alexander Wright had a son, John, christened in Oct 1723 in St. Ninians, Stirling, so John would be 38 at the time of the scandal.

---

[4] A 'change house' was a place for changing horses on coaches or wagons, usually an inn

The Hangman's Hungry Wife

3rd November 1762

Now here's an interesting situation ... Can you ask the Hangman to punish his own wife?

William McAlaister, commander of the Town Guards the previous night, reported -

'... that there had been a theft committed last night by some persons in the house of Widow Young, and the guard being applied to search the Hangman's house, they found one Jean Taylor from Torbrex, and the Hangman's wife, and on search found the shirts that had been stolen and nine bottles of ale and some cheese that had also been stolen, and that he had secured the said two women in the guard, and they being brought and examined, Jean Taylor acknowledges that on Saturday she and the hangman's wife had stolen a gallon of ale from Widow Young, and yesternight they stole from thence the shirts, ale and cheese above mentioned, and acknowledges that she is the same person that was banished this county for theft the twelfth of July last, and Isabel Canker the hangman's wife denied the theft, but owned that the other woman Taylor brought to her the ale and others foresaid, which being considered by the magistrates they of new banish the said Jean Taylor this town ... and ordains Jean Taylor to be whipped through the town by the hands of the Hangman receiving the usual number of stripes at the accustomed places upon her naked back, betwixt the hour of eleven and twelve forenoon, and continues advising us to the other woman till then, and appoints both of them to be carried back to the workhouse.'

Sadly, we're not informed as to what became of the Hangman's wife!

Prior to becoming Mrs Hangman, Isabel's life was far from innocent. At one point she stole some clothing from the area around the north side of Linlithgow Bridge. As that particular side of the Bridge fell under Stirling's jurisdiction, she was brought to the Tolbooth in Broad Street. It was there she met Jock Rankine – the Stirling Hangman. Well, Isabel and Jock were smitten. Love blossomed, and the day of her release was also the day of their marriage. Meanwhile, this unlikely affair had caught the town's imagination, and they were given a rousing turn-out on their big day. Four fully-dressed Town Officers accompanied them as they went to seal their union, and they were married by Provost Jaffray (a Justice of the Peace) in his full official regalia.

The course of true love did not run smoothly, however, and the couple went on to lead a cat-and-dog life. After one particularly ferocious quarrel, Jock was so incensed with rage he gulped down his supper a tad too hastily, and choked to death on a bone in his soup.

Bunton's Bottles

Case 20   **18th August 1763**

Janet, dear, you were given your chance, but you really are your own worst enemy –

Janet Bunton had been imprisoned in the Tolbooth since the 22nd of July due to some unspecified crime against a Mr James Lyon, shoemaker in Stirling, until she could find her own bail money, or 'caution'. She seemed quite unable to raise any money, however, saying she was

'in a starving condition and unable to find such caution',

but was willing to voluntarily banish herself. James Lyon agreed to this.

A mere five weeks later, *The Vagabond Book* notes with some annoyance that Janet felt unable to live up to her part of the bargain –

'Janet Bunton … continued to reside within the Burgh in contempt of the Magistrates authority, and to the offence of many, and being guilty of sundry abuses to some of the inhabitants, for which she was committed to the Workhouse the 16th Sept … she is to be conveyed by the town officers with their halberds[5] and the drum beating to the Port of Stirling bareheaded …'

And if she dares to return again?

' …   to be committed to the Workhouse at hard labour for 3 months, and be publicly whipped through the town the first Friday of each month and be again banished under more severe certifications …'

---

[5] A weapon with a steel spike and axe blade mounted on the end of a long shaft.

This is not the last we hear of Janet, though. She turns up again eleven years later, in June 1774 ...

'Christian McNab, a beggar woman and residenter in St. Ninians ... guilty of stealing 9 empty Chopin[6] bottles out of a cellar belonging to James Alexander, Provost of Stirling, ... acknowledged she did yesterday afternoon steal the aforesaid nine bottles from Provost Alexander's Cellar Door, six whereof she sold to James Campbell, brewer in Mary's Wynd at a penny per piece which he paid her, and the other three bottles were taken from her by Janet Bunton, residenter in Stirling, who was in the knowledge of said theft and advised the declarant to commit it, acknowledges that she was several years past banished from this burgh for malpractices then committed ...'

'Janet Bunton declares she has been acquainted for some time past with Christian McNab, and that she is a beggar, that she yesterday found the said McNab in the back part of the long passage or close immediately below the shop door of John Paterson, Tobacconist, near to head of Baxter Wynd,

Baxters Wynd was, as the name suggests, a street with many bakers. Today it is still known as Baker Street.

'that she observed McNab go into said close while she the declarant was on the street a little below, and upon coming up with her at the back shop door, she saw 3 empty Choppin bottles which the declarant took from her, alleging the bottles had been stolen and she carried them with her up the street, and she openly in the street as she passed from the above close asked who would

---

[6] half a Scots pint

buy the bottles from her, and on her getting to the foot of the Broad street the servant maid of Doctor Graham challenged the bottles and took them from her ...'

Broad Street

'... and the Baillie having considered the declarations, and that it appears upon record that the forenamed Janet Bunton was twice in the months of August and September, 1763 banished this Burgh and Territories thereof in all time thereafter for sundry malpractices, under high certifications, the Baillie of new banishes the said Janet Bunton and the forenamed Christian McNab, this Burgh and Territories thereof in all time coming with certification that if they or either of them be thereafter found within the same, they will be apprehended and imprisoned and be publickly whipt thro' the town of Stirling the first Friday of each of the two subsequent months by the hands of the common Hangman and be again banished under more severe certifications, and further the Baillie appoints the said Janet Bunton and Christian McNab to be immediately conveyed by Town Officers with their halberds without the burrows gate with the Staffman going behind the said delinquents with his whip in his hand.'

Now you might think she'd take the hint. But is she deterred? Oh no ...

4th August 1774

'Janet Bunton, mentioned in the immediate proceeding act of banishment, having returned to and been openly seen on the streets of this Burgh and on that account apprehended and recommitted to the Workhouse where she has since remained and being now brought before the Baillie, and that she

judicially acknowledges her having so returned to the Burgh notwithstanding the repeated Acts of Banishment standing against her ever since the 18th Aug 1763, the Baillie therefore appoints her to be recommitted to the Workhouse therein to remain till tomorrow until twelve o clock midday, and then betwixt that hour and one o clock afternoon to be carried prisoner by the Town Officers to the head of the Mercate Place at Mars Work there to have her head and shoulders uncovered, and her arms tied behind with a piece of rope, the end of which to be held in the Staffman's left hand and his whip in the other and from thence appoints her to be conducted down the principle streets of the burgh in the above manner to the Burrows Gate, the Officers also attending with their Halberts and the Town Drum beating behind her – and thereafter of new banishes her this Burgh and Territories thereof in all time coming with certification if she ever return she will be again committed to the Workhouse at hard labour until the first Friday after being apprehended and then publickly whipped through the Burgh by the hands of the common Hangman – and so often as she may thereafter return to the Burgh ordains her to be in like manner apprehended imprisoned and publickly whipped between the hours of twelve and one the Friday next after to her being apprehended, and this sentence is judicially read over and intimated to her.'

Provost James Alexander, who lost his bottles

This case centred around the theft and resale of bottles from Provost Alexander's cellar.

James Alexander was a grocer, wine and spirit merchant in Broad Street. Apparently he was always very neatly dressed, and could regularly be seen on a Friday afternoon carrying a pair of hens he'd bought for the pot.

He was a God-fearing man who observed the Sabbath, but had somehow acquired a talking cockatoo which, unfortunately, had picked up some choice and colourful expressions through associating with seafaring companions, and so consequently caused the good Provost acute embarrassment on Sundays.

Eventually, Provost Alexander was reduced to covering the bird's cage to stem the rich and unsavoury flow, while muttering fiercely "Wheesht – do ye ken what day this is?'

And now for something completely different. A wee bit of fiddling from the stores.

Alexander 'Del Boy' Noble

Case 21   **8th May 1775**

'Alexander Noble, found under night by the Town Guard in house in Castlehill behaving disorderly, and could give no satisfying account as to his character, and was found to have amongst other things in his custody a pair of new ammunition breeches[7] belonging to the Company of Invalids in Stirling Castle known to have been delivered out of the stores a few days past and believed to have been bought by him from one of the soldiers at an under value, but which he denies, alleging he bought them from William Johnstone in Castlehill in the presence of James Hamilton, soldier, to whom he afterwards understood they belonged, and for the said Alexander Noble having laid down on the table twenty pence as the price to Johnstone, Hamilton's wife then present took up sixpence thereof and Johnstone the rest, and Noble having now agreed to leave the above pair of breeches in the clerks custody for behoof of the garrison ...'

He's banished.

The 'Company of Invalids' up at Stirling Castle conjure up a sorry spectacle, but the term would mean something slightly different to today. These men were probably a mixture of those who were ill, convalescing, or recovering from wounds. All reasons for not being on active duty with their Regiments, although many of them would have been able to perform light duties such as guard duty – or manning the stores.

---

[7] guns

Now here's someone who might just attract your heartfelt sympathy.

He seems to have it in for the taxman.

Lurking Up the Custom Man's Close

Case 22   **31st January 1764**

'John McDougall, lately a soldier in Major McLean's Battalion of Foot, having about 3 months ago been detected in petty thefts and other transgressions, and having then verbally engaged to the persons wronged by him that he would immediately leave this place and never again return … and complaint being made against him by collector Dunbar, Collector of Excise, that McDougall had insulted the collector and given him abusive and threatening language and endeavoured to impose upon him and that McDougall was further discovered lurking in the Collectors close under cloud of night following the day foresaid, McDougall was carried to the Guard by order of a Magistrate.'

At least he admits he was previously banished, and promises to banish himself again.

Much to the relief of Mr Dunbar, we must assume. No-one likes finding a lurker up their close.

The Pilfered Pocketbook

Case 23   **31st July 1764**

'William Russell, tenant in Kersebonny, having complained that while he was in the Public Fair of Stirling this day about one of the clock in the afternoon, his pocketbook containing eighteen twenty shilling notes, two Glasgow ten shilling notes, and a Perth five shilling note, and a discharge, a receipt of rents from Provost John Gillespie, and that he suspected the following persons who were this day at the Fair and drinking in the house of Archibald McArthur, and upon a search of the officers endeavoured to run off, and some of their companions did make their escape.'

A Perth five-shilling note???

Believe it or not, this case highlights an interesting episode in Scottish banking history – a period when small individual town banks simply printed their own banknotes.

Early in the 18th century, two banks held the monopoly of major financial transactions – the Bank of Scotland, and the Royal Bank of Scotland, both based in Edinburgh. (The Bank of Scotland either had no clue at all how to raise capital, or had one of the first shrewd marketing strategies ever – they casually left a ledger in the nearby Cross Keys Inn to attract their first investors.)

Eventually, though, this geographical emphasis on Edinburgh became too inconvenient for provincial merchants, who joined forces to set up their own banks in major towns and cities.

Banknote of the Stirling Banking Company

(Photo courtesy of the Stirling Smith Art Gallery and Museum)

The notes of the Stirling Banking Company were validated by three signatures: Ebenezer Connal, James MacEwan, and James Eadie.

In 1818, a 22 year old woman appeared at Glasgow Circuit Court accused of passing forged guinea notes. Connal and Eadie were called as witnesses …

'Ebenezer Connal has been twelve years acting as clerk to the Stirling Bank at Stirling; the notes of the Company are payable to witness, and his name is always written on the notes by himself. Mr Eadie, late cashier, also, while he was cashier, put his name to the notes. James M'Ewan, who enters them, put his name to them likewise; seven of the notes described in the indictment were shown to the witness, who swore that all of them were cast from a forged plate, and that all the names on them were also fabricated. John Telford, the present cashier, corroborated the above evidence. James Eadie, residing in Stirling, was cashier to the Stirling Bank for six years prior to Martinmas last. He corroborated the evidence of Messrs Connal and Telford as to the forgery of the notes, and added, that the Bank had no notes bearing the dates or numbers of those exhibited.'

Despite the fact the accused was a poor homeless widow, the court showed no mercy.   She was sentenced to death.

The very first banknotes were bound in a small book, and notes were cut or ripped out as required. Any note could simply be torn into halves or quarters to represent smaller sums.   Some local banks, however, issued complete notes of very small values, such as the Perth 5/- note which vanished along with the pilfered pocketbook of William Russell.

Some confusion could arise, too, regarding the value of the Scottish pound versus the English.   An old story tells of a Stirling blacksmith – James Callendar - who worked up at the castle during the reign of King James VI. When the King succeeded to the throne of England in 1603, he not only left Stirling for London, he left his smith's bill unpaid, too. Callender was not best pleased, and set out on foot in pursuit of his money. The long trudge south turned out to be well worth his while. When Callendar eventually caught up with James in London, the King ordered his Treasurer to pay up. He did – but quite naturally paid in his local English currency, Pounds Sterling – worth an eye-watering twelve times more than Pounds Scots.

I think we can safely assume James Callendar's journey home was made with a much lighter step than his journey down.

Callendar eventually bought the local Craigforth estate, no doubt helped by his sudden influx of wealth.

The Abandoned Child

Case 24   **3rd August 1764**

Well now, what would today's social services have to say about this?

'Ann Robertson, apprehended on suspicion of being one of the gang of Gipsies or vagrants presently prisoners in Stirling Tollbooth being brought before the Justice and examined declares that she is daughter of John Robertson shoemaker in Edinburgh, deceased, that she is the spouse of John Thomson, soldier in the Reg. of Foot in Ireland called the Scottish Regiment, all now in Ireland, that she lives in Falkirk in a house rented from Robert Turner, change keeper, that she came to Stirling this day on her way to Kippen to see Robert Thomson, weaver there, her friend.

Having a child of a year old in her arms and that no person came from Falkirk to Stirling with her, declares that her child falling asleep in her arms, she left it in a house in this town, which she does not know neither knows she any of the persons living therein until the child should awake, and came down the street by the Tolbooth Wynd, when she saw a crowd looking at the vagrant prisoners in the Tolbooth, and that while she was looking at them also she was apprehended and brought to this place to be examined, and that she knows not any of these vagrants nor ever saw them, and the said Ann Robertson being sent with two constables to find the above house and child they returned with the child who was left in the house as she before had declared.'

The Justice dismisses her, but warns if she's *'found in this town or county without sufficient cause she will be committed to the correction house and punished as a vagrant'*.

The Tolbooth and Mercat Cross

The original Tolbooth was built between 1702-4. The old Tolbooth prison, however, was notoriously insecure. Hard liquor could easily be passed through the cell window to a prisoner, and at one stage the masonry was so bad the prisoners' work-tools were banned for fear they could simply chip straight through into the street.

Stirling Tolbooth

In 1785 the Tolbooth was extended, and further enlarged between 1806 and 1811 when a jail and courthouse were added. In all, the building would have contained The Town Clerk's office and the Council Chambers, along with the Sheriff Court and Jail.

Immediately outside stood the Tron - the town's official weighing-beam – and the Mercat Cross.

Most of the Stirling markets were held here. Criminals were displayed here, too, along with the odd public hanging.

Detail of Mercat Cross

A Bad Attack of The Staggers

Case 25   **17th April 1765**

How's this for a lame excuse?

'William Robertson, Tinker in the west end of the Castle hill, Margaret Robertson, and Janet Robertson, his two daughters, who were on the 6th current apprehended by the Town Guard and committed prisoners to the Workhouse for having been that night found in the coalhouse belonging to Mr Graham of McLlewood, betwixt the hours of 11 and 12 that night …. William Robertson declares he was in the coalhouse the time foresaid, but that he was the worse of liquor and wanted to shun his daughters in order to get more of it, and having come to the door of the coalhouse, he put his hand to it and it being open or unlocht he stumbled in, and his two daughters having followed him, found him in the coalhouse and were endeavouring to help him home, when they were discovered by some of the neighbours, and Margaret and Janet Robertson do adhere to their fathers declaration, and they all three voluntarily agree to banish themselves … in all time coming …'

Aye, right.

The Tinkers

The politically correct term these days would probably be 'travelling people', as the original word has now acquired a negative connotation. But 'tinker' simply meant someone who worked with tin – a tinsmith – who were usually either Irish or native Scots.

More often than not they were literally 'travelling people', going from door-to-door mending pots and pans, as well as selling hand-crafted baskets and pegs.

Local farmers valued their labour at harvesting, too, along with their skill in the breeding and training of horses. They could also turn their hand to pearl-fishing.

Tinkers were often confused with Gypsies, who were also 'travelling people' selling odds-and-ends and 'tinkering', but who were nevertheless quite different in origins, culture and lifestyle.

Black Affronted

Case 26   **22ⁿᵈ January 1766**

Jean Anderson didn't take too kindly to her dirty linen being exposed to the public gaze, so she turned the tables on everyone by flouncing off in a flurry of self-righteous indignation –

'Jean Anderson, washerwoman in Stirling, was upon the 21ˢᵗ December last committed prisoner to the Work-house for and on account of her pledging or disposing of some clothes belonging to Miss Bachop, with which she was entrusted for washing.'

Well, Jean stood up for herself. She told the Baillie in no uncertain terms there was no previous stain whatever on her character, but now -

'... that as her character had thereby suffered she could not live longer in the place with any reputation, and declared ... for that reason she was willing to leave the town of Stirling and not to return thereto in time coming ...'

This moral high ground was occupied yet again the next year –

17ᵗʰ August 1767

'Elizabeth Barclay, widow of the deceast John Stewart, Gildbrother of this Burgh, having been on the evening of Friday the 14ᵗʰ current committed by one of the magistrates to the Tollbooth of Stirling for disturbing her neighbours, behaving very indecently herself, and entertaining bad company in her house, and she, rather than stand trial for these offences, and that after such accusations she cannot live with any reputation in the place ...'

She voluntarily banishes herself.

Guilds

At least Elizabeth was the widow of a 'Gildbrother of this Burgh', and as such should never have found herself completely destitute.

Most of the major trades of the day – bakers, weavers, fleshers, etc., were organised into Guilds for mutual support and protection.

Their aims were to make sure only qualified craftsmen offered their trade to the burgh, so maintaining a high standard of quality.

All well and good, but the downside was that Guilds were effectively a closed shop, setting prices, crushing competition and enjoying monopolies. If you were a member, however, you were unlikely to starve on the streets.

John Cowane

Guilds collected money from their members to be used to relieve poverty in times of illness or bereavement, providing a lifeline for their widows and children. Many also ran their own almshouses.

Cowane's Hospital

In Stirling, Cowane's Hospital is a good example of such a scheme. Back in the 17th century, John Cowane, then Dean of Guild, left money to build a home for 'twelve 'decayed Guildbreithers' of the burgh.

Rumour suggests that the building stood empty for a while.

No Stirling merchants were prepared to admit they'd fallen on hard times.

THIS HOSPITALL
WAS ERECTED AND
LARGLY PROVYDED
BY IOHN COWANE
DEANE OF GILD FOR
THE ENTERTAINEMENT
OF DECAYED GILD
BRETHER

IOHN ✕ COWANE

Frenzy at the Fleshmarket

Case 27   **4th November 1766**

Ah, the delightful days of the Stirling Fairs, when all manner of things could be bought at the stalls, and much food and drink was consumed by all.

Sadly, things turned a bit sour for Ann and Helen, and it's a pity we'll never know what led to their argument. Sounds as if Helen definitely came off worse, though.

'*... One who calls herself Helen Campbell, relict of John Campbell, soldier in Lord Charles Manners Reg. of Foot, and Ann Wilson, who says that is her name, and that she is wife of Andrew Wilson, Tinker in Thornhill, having been brought before the Baillie on account of there having been the occasion of a Tumult and Mob in the Fleshmarket of Stirling, this afternoon being one of the old fairs of this burgh, in time of public Mercate, to the great disturbance of the Fair and Mercate, and they having both owned that this day in the Flesh Mercate of Stirling in time of open fair, they assaulted, fought, beat, bruised and abused one another to the effusion of blood, and the blood appearing in court on the face and head of Helen Campbell, the Baillie appoints both the said persons to be committed to the workhouse at hard labour till further examination.*'

Two days later the Baillie liberates them, but ...

'*... if they be found or either of them in any quarrel or theft within the burgh, they will immediately be committed to the workhouse at hard labour till liberated in due course of law.*'

The Flesh Market

In 1779 it was decided the 'Flesh Mercate' should be removed from the open street (between St. John Street and the Back Walk).

A large enclosed quadrangle was then purpose-built for the market, along with a slaughterhouse and stalls for the fleshers to sell their produce.

Site of old Flesh Market

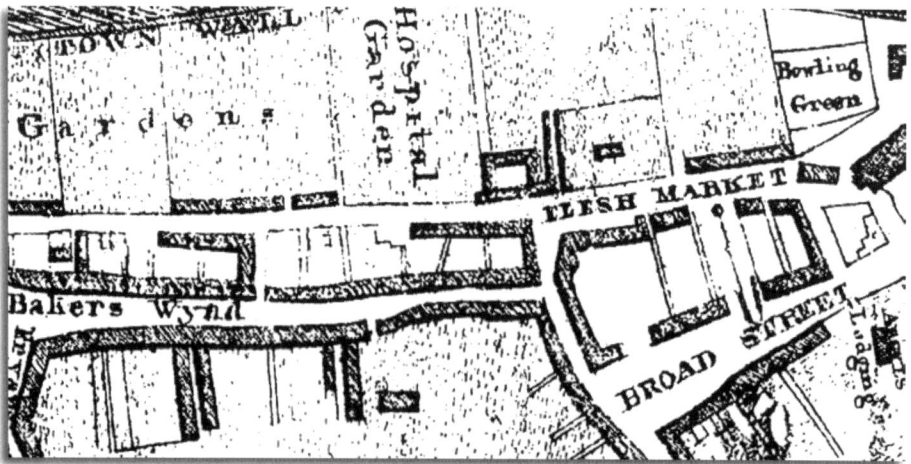

A rather quaintly-built tavern stood in the middle of the south side of St. John Street, primarily to cater for the thirst of the fleshers.

Fleshers' Tavern:
  very popular on Market days.

Very possibly popular on other days, too

A Meal Market was also held at the bottom of Baker Street.

This was eventually replaced by Corn Exchange Square - still acknowledged today in the name "Corn Exchange Road".

All outsiders with goods to sell had to pay a customs charge at the town gates.

Then, the main entry into Stirling was the enormous 'Barras Yett'[8] in Port Street– where the Dumbarton Road traffic lights are now.

Dumbarton Road/Port Street

This was demolished in the 1770s, although a Customs House still operated nearby. *The Port Customs Bar* on the nearby corner still bears testimony to this area's long-vanished history.

For those in the know, there are plaques on both the wall and pavement showing the site of the old Burgh Gate.

You'll find them just to the right of the carved statue.

Dumbarton Road ...

---

[8] a gate in or beside a barrier

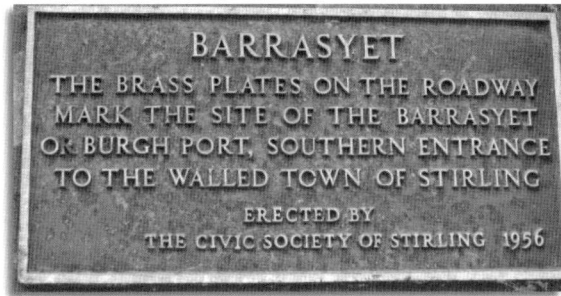

... Wall plaque

... and pavement insert

The site of the New Port Gate is also marked out on the stones in the middle of King Street, near to the Golden Lion Hotel. Gates were also erected at other strategic routes into the town, namely the Bridge Port, Mary Wynd Port and Friar Wynd Port.

An official was usually in evidence at each of the town's markets, checking produce to ensure correct weights were being sold. One very old story concerns a woman selling butter who was picked out for a random check. She knew she was selling underweight goods, so in a panic she pressed a half-crown piece into the middle of the butter to make it heavier. So far, so good - but someone in the crowd noticed her deception and immediately asked to buy that particular round of butter. To protest would look suspicious and lead to awkward questions, so rather than draw attention to herself she grimly parted company with both her butter **and** her half-crown.

Even with the best intentions, though, things could go badly wrong between merchant and customer. One well-to-do lady, hearing of her sister's illness, immediately made plans to travel to her bedside. She ordered the largest chaise that could be found.

Imagine her expression when two men arrived at her door, red-faced and out of breath, staggering under the weight of an enormous cheese.

Drummond the Drummer Drummed

Case 28   **19ᵗʰ December 1767**

Who will drum out Drummond, the Drummer? As ever, it's the woman who's punished …

'Mary Canker from Lithgow who was upon the 17ᵗʰ current committed prisoner to the Tolbooth of Stirling, upon a warrant from the Provost, for behaving in an indecent manner with James Drummond, the Town Drummer, and otherways behaving ill during the night foresaid … voluntarily agreed to banish herself … and Margaret Douglas, daughter of James Douglas, weaver in Stirling, who was formerly banished the Burgh, and convened for the same fault as Mary Canker the night foresaid, … also voluntarily agreed to banish herself again …'

Lithgow, incidentally, was an old name for Linlithgow.   And was Mary the sister of Isabel Canker, the Hangman's wife?   It's certainly possible – a George Canker and Janet Dalrymple christened a daughter Isabel in Linlithgow in 1729, followed in 1735 by a daughter Mary.

From Blair Drummond to the Burgh Gate

Case 29   **14ᵗʰ August 1771**

Agnes' petty misdemeanours started off in distinguished enough company, then rapidly slid down the social scale …

'Agnes McKenzie, who has been for sometime past confined in the workhouse on account of her abstracting from the house of Blair Drummond some Table Napery, and voluntarily banishes herself.'

... but by 14th November -

'Agnes McKenzie having been lately found in company with some lewd persons and committed to the Workhouse, to be conveyed by the Officers with their Halberds to the burrows gate with the Drum beating, she being bare headed – and afterwards banished for all time coming.'

Now a wee bit of serious history. Pop the kettle on, have a cup of tea, and come back in five minutes if you're not interested. But if you've ever heard of Blair Drummond or the Carse of Stirling, you'll want to read on ...

Blair Drummond and Flanders Moss

Blair Drummond Estate lies 4 miles north-west of Stirling, and is now best associated with the Blair Drummond Safari and Adventure Park. Before 1766, though, the surrounding land was almost entirely moss-covered peat bog, totally useless for cultivation, even though the land underneath was extremely fertile.

Flanders Moss

Although most locals in the know could pick their way safely through the bog, legend would like to suggest Rob Roy was at one time the *only* person who could find his way across.

Previous attempts to clear the moss had been made, but they were piecemeal and very localised. But by 1766, the new owner, Lord Kames, initiated a scheme so comprehensive, imaginative and far-seeing it transformed the landscape forever.

Lord Kames, incidentally, was no mere landed gentry up at the Big Hoose. He was a leading light of the Scottish Enlightenment, and a Law Lord to boot.

49

Kames reasoned that the easiest way to clear the moss was to use the existing water in the bog to his advantage. Just cut a three-mile channel straight through the Carse of Stirling, chop the peat and moss into chunks – then simply float them down the artificial watercourse to the River Forth! Well, that was the theory. But would it work? Who would do it? He had an equally ingenious solution. He offered prospective labourers a lease of a portion of land on his estate, along with wood to help build a house and a year's supply of oatmeal. Not only that, the first seven years were to be rent-free. All the workforce had to do in return was clear the peat from their portion of land.

The project grew so that by 1811 over 750 people lived in and around the Moss, their homes made from blocks of the peat bog they worked on, with turf and timber roofs. There were precious few comforts, especially as most of the work was carried out during the cold, raw winter months, when water levels were higher than in summer.

The work itself must have been back-breaking. One tenant cleared eleven acres of land, using only his bare hands, a wheelbarrow, and a spade. The wet peat was about four metres deep, and weighed almost 91,000 metric tons.

For those of you who prefer to measure things in elephants, that's the equivalent of 11,195 very large African bulls.

After Kames died in 1783 his son George took up the project. But now, strangely enough, the land was even more difficult to clear as the remaining peat was much more densely packed due to becoming compressed by the weight of the top layer.

George must have inherited his father's inventiveness, for he quickly reasoned the more difficult the labour required, the hardier the people needed to complete it. And who else but big, strong, burly Highlanders, who had recently been evicted from their own homes and land due to the Clearances? (Most of the labour, in fact, came from the Perthshire Highlands, from places such as Glen Lyon or Balquhidder.)

To help their efforts, a huge water wheel was built beside the River Teith, channelling the flushed peat through a network of ditches out to the River Forth. The local salmon fishers were not best pleased. The people downstream at Culross, on the other hand, were delighted. They promptly fished it out again and used it as fertiliser.

In total, around 850 hectares of land was cleared, leaving the underlying rich clay soil to be cultivated as farmland.

Flanders Moss: close-up of bog

Today, the Carse of Stirling is considered one of the most fertile areas of Scotland, and the remaining uncleared bog of Flanders Moss is now a National Nature Reserve of considerable significance for conservation and study.

Farmland at edge of Flanders Moss

The Banished Baillies of "The Black Bond"

Round about this point in The Vagabond Book there is a gap of six years. Did the inhabitants of Stirling suddenly wake up one fine morning with a song on their lips, their hearts brimming with goodwill, and decide to become model citizens? As theories go, it's certainly one possible explanation. Hardly a likely one, though.

A more probable reason for this hiatus may be indirectly related to the political scandal which rocked the town in the 1770s, causing disruption to normal Council activities. In 1771 a letter came to light exposing the utter corruption of those in high office within the Town Council. Written jointly by James Burd, Henry Jaffray and James Alexander, the letter – styled **"The Black Bond"** - showed they had agreed to elect mutual friends to prominent positions, to *'weaken the interest of Nicol Bryce and by degrees to exclude him and his friends from the council altogether ...'*

Those elected would, of course, pay a sum of money for the privilege, which would be shared between the three ringleaders. Even worse, the three in question were happy to lend their considerable weight to influence parliamentary elections – again for a substantial fee.

Another nice little earner came by way of the Town Clerk. In 1766, John McGibbon was appointed to the post, but after a few years became somewhat infirm, and arranged with the "Black Bonders" to install his son – a mere callow youth – as his assistant and successor. In return, £25 a year would be taken from his salary, and divided between the three instigators.

The main ringleader appears to be Baillie James Burd, Maltster and Merchant, *'a man more feared than respected'*, according to one pithy observer of local affairs, who went on to suggest -

'In his care his ancestral nobility had undergone a significant metamorphosis – the fine gold had become valueless dross.'

He was rumoured to be such an unpleasant and overbearing character that one of his servant-girls jumped from Stirling Bridge and drowned herself. Her body floated to the surface several days later, coming to rest, with some poetic justice, on a patch of land rented out to Burd himself.

The third participator in the conspiracy was Provost James Alexander, grocer, wine and spirit merchant, Broad Street, whom we have met before getting in a Sunday lather regarding the offensive language of his pet cockatoo.

In 1777, James, along with six others, originated The Stirling Banking Company. He is rumoured to have had a double share of the venture, so that his interest was proportionately greater. He soon bought up the shares of one or two of the other partners, too, and amassed some considerable wealth. One local worthy supplies us with this description:

'James Alexander was of a very facile disposition, but when stirred up to a certain point he proved a very determined character. He was a man of no great stature, always neat and trim in his dress, usually wearing a full skirted single breast snuff brown coloured coat; a long breasted waistcoat of same shade, his small clothes of drab casimere, and large well polished silver buckles in his shoes. His hair was tied in a cue hanging down his back and wore voluminous ruffles at his wrist sleeves.'

Things came to a head in 1773, when a group of burgesses finally had had enough, and went to the Court of Session demanding the ringleaders be removed from office.

The Court suspended the entire council in 1773, and later appointed Mr John Glass, merchant, Dr John Gillespie, physician, and David Gourlay, Esquire of Kippendarroch to manage the town's affairs, including choosing new magistrates.

The burgh's full rights were not fully reinstated until 1781. Which is exactly where The Vagabond Book begins recording again …

Not Quite All There

Case 30   **20th September 1781**

No disability allowance in those days, either …

'The following persons who were apprehended in the house of Janet Carmichael indweller in Stirling, who has been complained of as keeping a bad house, declared their names are as follows: James Campbell, Slater, last from Berwick, lame of an arm, Mary Clark his wife also wanting a hand, and their child, Benjamin [unreadable] from Dublin, lame of an arm, and Susanna Berkley (Barclay) his wife, David Smith, formerly Chaise driver in Edinburgh, lame of the right leg, Robert Johnston, an old soldier and Chelsea Pensioner from Edinburgh, and John Johnston his son … not being able to give a proper account of themselves …'

They're all banished.

'Thereafter Margaret McLean who says she is wife of Thomas Lindsay formerly a Slater who fell from a house and lamed himself and broke his back and goes through the country begging, Margaret Keith, wife of John Hamilton, travelling Chapman from Glasgow, Janet Hamilton, residing in Edinburgh and Janet Hamilton, daughter of Margaret Keith having been found strolling as vagrants and …not being able to give a proper account of themselves …'

They're all banished, too.

Going To Extreme Lengths

Case 31   **8th September 1783**

And here we have two people who take rather drastic action to avoid a trial.

'John Warran, journeyman weaver in Stirling who was guilty of riotous practices, and as being suspected of sundry petty thefts declares that he was once a soldier in the South Fencible Regiment from which he was discharged for being troublesome and insolent to his officers and that he is willing to banish himself and family furth of the Town in all time coming rather than go to trial.'

Case 32   **10th February 1786**

But that's nothing compared to the length Robert's prepared to go. Literally.

'Robert Davie, stocking maker in Stirling, present prisoner in the Tollbooth there for the crime of stealing and abstracting candles from the candle house of Mrs Littlejohn, merchant in Stirling, and for selling the same at an *undervalue. That he acknowledges himself guilty of the said crime, and to avoid the consequences of a trial willingly consented to banish himself this Country and Kingdom ... and that John Davie, father of Robert, would enact himself a caution for his son, that he should not only leave the place, but also this Kingdom immediately, and for that purpose he has procured a passage for his son in a vessel from Leith to London, and the magistrates further considering that the said Robert Davie had already suffered a severe imprisonment of 3 months, and that the Procurator Fiscal has consented to the said petition, provided the prisoner be banished for the space of 7 years, and that the prisoner being now brought before them judicially adhered to the said petition, and agreed that the term of his banishment should be extended to the foresaid space of 7 years or to what other term or time the magistrates should specify ...'*

And Finally ... The Cross-Dressing Criminal

Case 33   **13th November 1782**

The expression 'ending on a high' is not too morally appropriate in our case, so, in keeping with the rogues and vagabonds we've met, let's end on a new low ....

'Euphan Graham, widow of Charles Jamieson who was executed at Linlithgow Bridge some years ago, and Ann Wilson, daughter of Andrew Wilson a niece of James Wilson who was executed at Edinburgh some time ago having been apprehended at the Bridge of Stirling in company with James Jamieson, son of the said Charles Jamieson, and which James was dressed in women's clothes, ... are now ordained to be put out of the town with certifications if they be ever found here again they will be immediately imprisoned and preceeded against according to law, especially the said Euphan Graham as she was formerly banished, and she and said Ann Wilson have now engaged not to return to this town.'

Stirling Bridge

The Execution of Charles Jamieson

Charles Jamieson and his brother-in-law were leaders of a notorious gypsy band of thieves and robbers. In 1770 they were finally apprehended and brought to justice before an Edinburgh court. Both were sentenced to execution at Linlithgow Bridge. So apprehensive were the authorities of some daring escape plan that every available armed man was called upon to stand guard. As night fell, the whole town went into lock-down. All entry points to the town were closed, with the result that visitors from the neighbouring town of Bo'ness couldn't return home, and were forced to stay in Linlithgow overnight.

It worked. No rescue attempt was made, and the following morning

'All was peace and silence throughout the immense crowd surrounding the gallows, patiently waiting the appearance of the criminals. In due time the condemned made their appearance, in a cart, accompanied by Charles and James Jamieson, two youths, sitting beside their father and uncle, busily eating rolls, and, to all appearance, totally indifferent to the fate of their relatives, and the awful circumstances surrounding them.'

The reality of his fate was not lost on Jamieson, who seemed suitably unnerved. His brother-in-law, however, remained cocksure till the last, nonchalantly chewing tobacco and spitting out the juice with an air of contempt.

As the executioner prepared to dispatch them, the condemned man turned to him, dropped some money into his hand, and said *'Now, John, don't bungle your job.'* Moments later, both men dropped from the scaffold.

Did they rest in peace? They most certainly did not. The gypsies buried them in a moor outside Linlithgow, but the magistrates ordered them to be exhumed and re-interred in the east end of Linlithgow churchyard, only for the outraged local populace to dig the bodies up again and bury them – for the third and final time - in a neighbouring field.

The Jamieson family notoriety didn't end there. Both young Charles and James were executed in 1786 for robbing the Kinross mail. When the facts of the case came to light, our Stirling magistrates must have breathed a long sigh of relief that they had sent them packing four years earlier. Nothing compared to the relief the local Stirling post-boys must have felt, though ...

While planning the robbery, James' mother, Euphan Graham, insisted that the post-boy should never be allowed to identify them. He should be murdered.

Charles and James refused. They then came to an agreement they should attack him in the stable yard of the inn where the coach usually stopped. This was done, but the criminals were pursued and soon tracked down to a house near Stirling.

They were eventually overpowered and arrested, but not before one desperately tried to escape by climbing up the chimney. That having failed, they both set about the officers with knives. They used their teeth, too.

Charles and James were executed.

Euphan Graham was said to have been transported.

The End

Sources:

Cameron, Joy. *Prisons and Punishment in Scotland: from the Middle Ages to the Present.* Edinburgh: Canongate, 1983.

Cant, Ronald G. and Lindsay, Ian G. *Old Stirling.* Edinburgh: Oliver and Boyd, 1948.

Drysdale, William. *Auld Biggins of Stirling.* Stirling: Eneas Mackay, 1904.

Fleming, J S. *Old Nooks of Stirling.* Stirling: Munro & Jamieson, 1898.

Fleming, J. S. *The Old Ludgings of Stirling.* Stirling: Eneas Mackay,1897.

King, Elspeth. *Old Stirling.* Stirling: Stenlake Publishing, 2009.

Lannon, Tom. *The Making of Modern Stirling.* Stirling: Forth Naturalist & Historian, Stirling University, 1983.

Lindsay, Elma. *Stirling: a stroll down memory lane.* Stirling: Stirling District Libraries, 1995.

Mair, Craig. *Stirling: the Royal Burgh.* Edinburgh: John Donald, 1995.

McKean, Charles. *Stirling and the Trossachs.* Edinburgh: RAIS/Scottish Academic Press, 1985.

McNaughton, Duncan. *A History of Old Stirling.* Stirling: Stirling Council Educational Resources Unit, 1980.

Mitchison, Rosalind. *The Old Poor Law in Scotland: the experience of poverty, 1574-1845.* Edinburgh: Edinburgh University Press, 2000.

Plant, Marjorie. *The Domestic Life of Scotland in the 18th Century.* Edinburgh: Edinburgh University Press, 1952.

Ronald, James. *Landmarks of Old Stirling.* Stirling: Eneas Mackay, 1899.

Shearer's Stirling: Historical and Descriptive. Stirling: R. S. Shearer & Son, 1897.

Shirra, James. *Various manuscripts*, At: Stirling Central Library, Stirling.

The Vagabond Book of Stirling: 1752-1787, At: Stirling Archives, Stirling.

For further information on Stirling Archives and their holdings, see Stirling Council's official website:

http://www.stirling.gov.uk/index/accessinformation/archives.htm

INDEX